Folens
Religious Education

C000075660

Contents

Daily Life
Lifestyles   2-3
Christianity: Sister Kathleen   4-5
Judaism: A day of rest   6-7

Festivals
Celebration: A time to remember   8-9
Christianity: Lent   10-11
Judaism: Purim   12-13

Community
Working together   14-15
Christianity: The parish   16-17
Judaism: Jewish communities   18-19

Places
Special places   20-21
Christianity: Cathedrals   22-23
Judaism: Israel   24-25

Story
The story of Esther   26-28
When Jesus was crucified   29-31

What have you learned?   32

Christine Moorcroft

Lifestyles

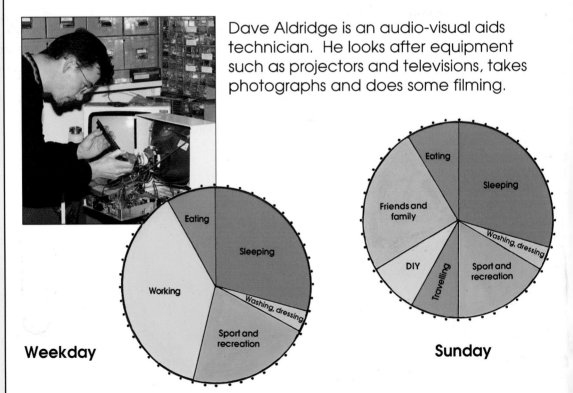

Sue Tyndall is a secretary. She works from Monday to Friday in a college. The charts show what she did on one weekday and on Sunday.

Weekday

Relaxing
With children
Travelling
Housework and preparing meals
Sleeping
Washing, dressing, eating, shopping
Working

Sunday

Relaxing
With children
Housework and preparing meals
Sleeping
At church
Washing, dressing, eating, shopping

Dave Aldridge is an audio-visual aids technician. He looks after equipment such as projectors and televisions, takes photographs and does some filming.

Weekday

Eating
Working
Sleeping
Washing, dressing
Sport and recreation

Sunday

Eating
Friends and family
DIY
Travelling
Sleeping
Washing, dressing
Sport and recreation

1   With a partner, list the things that Sue and Dave **have** to do and those that they do because they **want** to.

2   Explain any differences between their weekdays and Sundays.

3   Plan a survey to find out how people spend a typical weekday, Saturday and Sunday.

4   Record your findings. Make a diary for each person.

Name			
	Weekday	Saturday	Sunday
Morning			
Afternoon			
Evening			

You may need to change these times. Remember, do not speak to strangers.

Which activities serve other people?

Which activities serve God?

5   Talk to a partner about the activities of the people in your survey.

Which are just for the person himself or herself?

6   Classify the activities by using a chart like this:

	Serving others	Serving God	Serving self
Have to do			
Want to do			

7   Talk to a partner about your own activities and classify them in a similar way.

8   Which do you spend most time on, working or relaxing:
- on Sundays?
- on weekdays?
- on Saturdays?

Explain the differences.

Working	Relaxing

So ... what have you learned about how much time people spend thinking about their religion?

Sister Kathleen is a Roman Catholic nun. She works as a lecturer, training student teachers.

1 How can you tell from the photographs that Sister Kathleen is a nun?

2 Why does she wear a cross?

Look at how Sister Kathleen spends some of her time.

3 Compare this to the diaries of people in your survey on page 3.

4 Compare it to the way the people on page 2 spend their time.

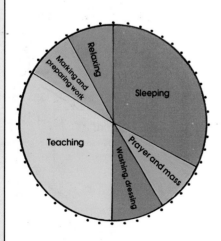

Weekday

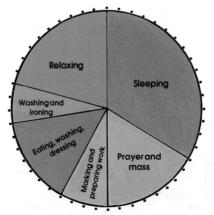

Sunday

Sister Kathleen lives with other nuns of the Notre Dame order.

The photograph shows the sisters just before a meal.

5   Explain what they are doing.

6   Why do some Christians do this before meals?

7   In groups, talk about prayers before meals. Then write
          your own prayer to be spoken before a special meal.

Think about ...

... how you will begin,
          ... who you are talking to,
               ... what you are thankful for,
                    ... how you will finish the prayer.

> *What could you give thanks for, as well as for food?*

8   Describe what you will do while you are praying.

9   Explain why you will do these things.

10   Does everyone in the group do the same thing?
          If not, why?

**So ... what have you learned about how nuns show
          devotion to God and about prayer?**

The photographs show four different meanings for 'work' and 'rest'.

 1 Which photographs show work and which show rest? Copy and complete the chart.

2 Explain your answers.

Picture	Work or rest?
a	
b	
c	
d	

There are 39 types of work, called melachot, which Jews are forbidden to do on Shabbat (Sabbath), their day of rest.

 3 Find out what these forbidden activities are and how they came to be forbidden.

4 Which of the activities in the four pictures are forbidden on Shabbat? Explain your answers.

5 In groups, talk about how you would feel about being forbidden to do these things, once a week.

Shabbat is a holy day that is welcomed joyfully each week by Jews. The Shabbat meal is a special one, prepared on Friday, before sunset. Shabbat begins at sunset on Friday and ends at sunset on Saturday.

In the picture, the mother has just lit the candles to welcome Shabbat. The family are about to begin their special Shabbat meal.

6 How do you think the family feel?

7 Describe the things in the picture that show this meal is different from an ordinary meal.

The Shabbat bread is called challah. The plural is challot.

8 Look at recipe books to find out how challah is different from ordinary bread.

9 Find out about the story of the Israelites in the wilderness. You can read it in the Book of Exodus. Explain how the challot commemorate this story.

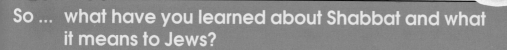

So ... what have you learned about Shabbat and what it means to Jews?

Celebration

The photograph shows a happy carnival scene.

  1   How is carnival day different from ordinary days?
Copy and complete the chart.

Actions	Clothes	Food	Decorations	Sounds

2   How do people feel at festival time? Think about any
carnivals, festivals or fairs that you have been to.

Describe feelings: before the festival (preparing)
during the festival (taking part)
after the festival (getting back
to normal).

In Britain the poppy is used as a symbol to remember people who have died in wars. It was chosen because so many were growing in the fields of Northern France, where many soldiers died during the First World War.

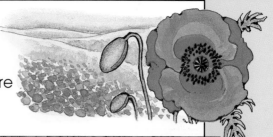

The photograph shows a Remembrance Day service on 11th November, when people wear poppies.

3 Describe the differences between this festival and the carnival.

4 Find out about a sad event that happened near where you live.

5 Describe how the event is remembered.
- What do people do?
- Has anything been built?
- Are any symbols used?

So ... what have you learned about different kinds of celebrations and how they are remembered?

Christianity

Lent begins on Ash Wednesday and lasts for 40 days until Easter. The day before Ash Wednesday is Shrove Tuesday. 'Shrove' comes from a medieval word: 'shriven'. This means to be forgiven for sins that have been confessed.

Shrove Tuesday   **Ash Wednesday**

Many Christians go to Ash Wednesday church services. The priest puts ashes on their foreheads. These are a symbol to show that a person is trying to think of God rather than everyday things and will try to do good in the future.

1   Decide what day the words in **A** describe. Sort them using a copy of the chart. Which words could describe both pictures?

A

Fun
Thoughtful
Quiet
Noisy
Caring
Enjoying
Peaceful
Lively
Happy
Thinking of God
Thinking of self

Shrove Tuesday	Ash Wednesday

2   In groups, list some 'everyday' things that you could stop thinking about on Ash Wednesday.

3   Which would you find the most difficult to forget about?

4   Think of a good deed that you could do in the future. Talk to a partner about it.

Lent is a time when Christians remember the 40 days Jesus spent fasting in the wilderness. He thought only of God. You can read about it in the Bible in Matthew 4:1-11.

5 What is a wilderness like? Close your eyes and imagine it. Draw your wilderness.

6 Describe the sounds that you could hear there.

7 How would you feel if you were alone there?

List the things that you would think about in the wilderness.

Many Christians try to do without luxuries during Lent, just as Jesus gave up food for 40 days.

8 Find out about the luxuries enjoyed by others in your class. Are they things people really **need**, or are they just things people **want**?

9 Which luxury would you give up to help others?

10 Plan a way for your class to help others during Lent and at other times.

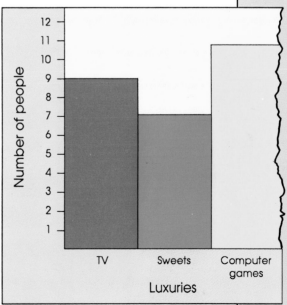

So ... what have you learned about why and how Christians celebrate Lent?

Purim is celebrated on the 14th day of the month of Adar in the Jewish calendar. This is usually in February or March. You can read more about the festival in the Bible in the Book of Esther.

1 Describe the festival of Purim as shown in the picture. Is it happy, sad, thoughtful, serious, lively, fun, noisy, quiet?

2 Read the story of Esther on pages 26-28.
In a group, plan and practise a short play about Esther, Haman and Mordecai. This planning chart may help.

Purim play notes:			
Characters	Story	Jokes	Costumes

3 Perform your play to another group.

Purim is a happy time. Make your audience laugh!

At Purim, some Jews give at least two portions of their food to friends and to poor people. Everybody gives and receives. Nobody is embarrassed to be given food.

Special pastries called Hamantaschen are made and eaten. They commemorate the banquet when Esther persuaded Haman not to kill the Jews.

MORDECHAI · HAMAN · QUEEN ESTHER · KING AHAZUERUS

PUPPETS FROM THE STORY OF THE BOOK OF ESTHER

4 Find out how to make Hamantaschen (Haman's pockets), to share with your friends at Purim.

5 Find out and explain why **A**, **B** and **C** below are described by Jews as 'Purims'.

A. Cairo 'Purim' 1524

An Egyptian Governor imprisoned 12 Jews and wanted a ransom for their release. He threatened to kill all Jews in Cairo if he was not paid. A servant stabbed him and the 12 Jews were set free.

B. Damascus 'Purim' 1743

The Governor of Damascus besieged Tiberius, where many Jews lived. They suffered for 83 days, but were finally saved.

C. Hitler 'Purim' 1942

The Jews of Casablanca were saved from Nazi invaders.

So ... what have you learned about the meaning of Purim, in the past and today?

A community is a group of people who have the same interests.

  1   Look at the photographs. How can members of a
community help each other?
Copy and complete this chart.

Community	Purpose	How the members can help each other
a		
b		
c		

2   With a partner, list some
communities that you know.

3   How do their members help
each other? Record your
findings on a chart like the
one above.

*What is the
purpose of these
communities?*

Community

Cities, towns and villages have public places which belong to everybody. Sometimes people spoil these places.

4 How have the places in the pictures been spoiled by people?

5 Why do some people not look after public places?

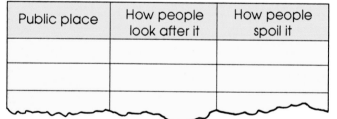

6 Find out about some public places near where you live. Copy and complete the chart below.

What could you and your friends do to help keep public places pleasant?

Public place	How people look after it	How people spoil it

7 Describe any times when you have seen someone spoiling a public place for others.

8 List some reasons why they do this.

So ... what have you learned about how you and other people can help each other?

Christian churches serve the people in their surrounding areas, or parishes.

   1   What do the people in this parish do together? Copy and complete the chart to help you organise your findings.

Age groups of people (M = Male, F = Female) (✔)											
under 5		5-11		11-16		16-21		21-60		over 60	
M	F	M	F	M	F	M	F	M	F	M	F

(Activity)

2   For which groups of people are there no activities? What activities could be organised for these groups?

   3   Find out about the parish in which your school is situated. Look at a map to find out how big it is.

> *Take this and eat; this is my body ... Drink from it, all of you. For this is my blood the blood of the covenant, shed for many for the forgiveness of sins.*
> (Mathew 26: 26-29)

4 Read the story 'When Jesus was crucified', on pages 29-31. Do you think Jesus knew what was going to happen to him? Explain your answer.

A

5 Look at **A**. Describe what is being used in the Holy Communion service.

6 Read the words of a Holy Communion prayer in **B**. Explain it.

7 Find out what many Christians believe they are sharing during Holy Communion.

B *Almighty God, our heavenly Father. We have sinned against our fellow men in thought, word and deed, through negligence, through weakness, through our own deliberate fault. We are truly sorry and repent of all our sins.*

So ... what have you learned about Christian ideas of serving others and of Holy Communion?

Some cities have large Jewish communities. These photographs show parts of a Jewish community.

1 How do you know that these four pictures show parts of a Jewish community?

2 Kosher means 'fit to eat'. Different people have different meanings for this. Talk about what 'fit to eat' or 'kosher' might mean to Jews.

3 Jewish children living in cities often have only Jewish friends from their community. How could parties and outings with any non-Jewish friends be difficult for them? Think about food, dates and times and weekends.

4 Find out about the 39 forbidden melachot (see page 6). Explain why it is useful for Jews to live near a synagogue.

Look at these pictures of a Jewish school. It is Friday, 10th December.

5   Talk about the pictures. Explain why the classroom has a lamp above the curtained alcove.

6   Explain why the children will go home at 2pm today.

Think about the words, letters and objects in the room.

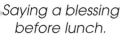

Saying a blessing before lunch.

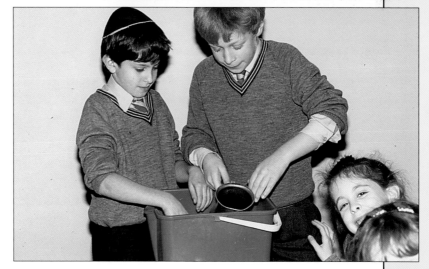

7   Describe what the children in the pictures are doing.

8   How is this school different from your school? How is it the same? Explain the differences.

So ... what have you learned about how Jewish belief can affect behaviour?

19

Places

Special places

Look at the photographs of places that people think are special.

 1 Decide what is special about these places. Copy and complete the chart.

Places can be special for many reasons:
a. *They hold beautiful things made by people.*
b. *Important decisions are made there.*
c. *People can go there for peace and quiet.*

Place	Why it is special
a	
b	
c	

2 Use photographs and books or magazines to find a place that is special for you.

3 Explain your choice to a partner. What makes it special?

...an and make a special ...lace in your school. Work with friends.

4 What is the special place for?

5 List some places where it could be made and decide which would be the best place.

6 Copy and use this chart to plan your special place.

Sketch what it will look like.	What it will sound like. (It could be silent.)
	How we will make the sounds, or make sure it is silent.
	Materials:

7 Talk about rules for using your special place.

How can we keep it special?

When can it be used?

Who will look after it?

Who can use it?

8 Write your rules in a way that makes them look special.

9 Make your special place.

So ... what have you learned about how to make and keep an ordinary place special?

Christianity

Cathedrals are holy places. They are often designed to show the importance of God, that He is here forever, but that people are on the Earth for only a short time.

1   What do you notice about the size of the cathedral in the picture?

2   Think of some enormous places where you have been. How did you feel when you were there?

3   How does this cathedral show the importance of God?

4   List parts you think were the most difficult to make. List parts you think are the most beautiful. Explain your answers.

When a cathedral is built, only the best architects are asked to design it. Only the most skilful crafts people work on the cathedral. They use the best quality materials. A cathedral is a holy place, where Christians pray. It is also a monument to the glory of God.

5 Explain why such care is taken in the building of a cathedral.

6 Work with a partner. Choose the photograph that you both think shows that a cathedral is a holy place. Explain why you think this.

7 Which photograph best shows the glory of God? Explain why you think this.

So ... what have you learned about why a cathedral is a special place of worship for Christians?

Judaism

The nation of Israel was created in 1948. Jews lived in Palestine over 3,000 years ago, but many times were driven out of their home towns and villages by others.   Eventually many settled, in groups, all over the world. Some remained in Israel.

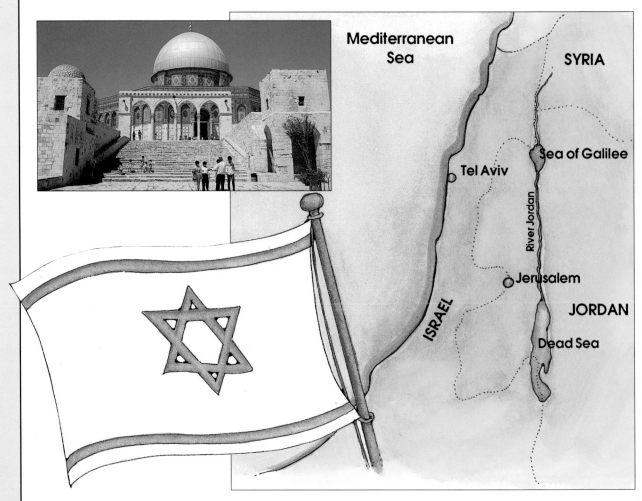

1   Imagine that you and your family were chased away from where you live. Describe how you would feel and what you would do.

2   If you had to go and live in a strange place, how would you feel if your way of life was very different from others?

3   Find out about the star on the flag. This is called the Magen David or shield of David.

4   Why do you think it was chosen for the emblem on the national flag?

Read these two passages from the Bible about the land of the Jewish people.

There the Lord appeared to Abraham, and said, "I give this land to your descendants."

(The Book of Genesis 12:7) The land was Canaan which covered part of Israel.

I will restore the fortunes of my people, Israel; they shall rebuild deserted cities and live in them, they shall plant vineyards and drink their wine, make gardens and eat the fruit.

(The words of God, in the Book of Amos 9:14)

Jews in some countries were forced to leave. They were attacked, and even killed. The words from the Bible, shown on this page, tell us about God's promises to the Jews.

5 Explain why Jews wanted to live in Israel.

6 Why do you think Jews have always had great faith that Israel would, once again, be theirs?

7 Find out more about Israel and explain how God's promises have been kept.

So ... what have you learned about why the land of Israel is so important to Jews?

There was once a mighty king called Ahasuerus. He ruled the great empire of Persia. Ahasuerus was very proud. He was so proud that he lost his wife, Queen Vashti.

It happened like this. A rule of the Persian court was that no one could speak to the king unless he said so. The king sat on his great throne with a golden sceptre in his hand. If he pointed the sceptre at you, then you were allowed to walk near to the throne. If he ordered you to appear before him, you had to. But Queen Vashti was proud. One day she refused to appear before the king. Ahasuerus was angry at her rudeness. She had disobeyed him and was sent away from the palace.

The years passed after this terrible event. Ahasuerus became lonely. He wanted to marry again. He ordered the unmarried women of his great empire to come to his palace, so that he could chose a new wife. Women rushed to the court. One of them was Esther. She was an orphan who had been looked after by her cousin, Mordecai. People said that there was something very special about Esther. When the king saw her for the first time he fell in love. "You will be my Queen," he said.

Esther was Jewish, but she did not tell the king. Jews have often lived among people who have hated them. This is why Esther kept her religion a secret from the king.

After Esther had been crowned queen, Mordecai, her cousin, came to the palace every day to see her. He wanted to be sure that she was happy. One day in the courtyard he passed Haman, the king's chief minister. Haman was a cruel man. He wanted everyone to show him respect by bowing to him. Mordecai was proud and he refused.

"How dare you insult me!" roared Haman. "You will suffer for this!" Haman promised to kill all the Jews in Persia. He went to the king.

"My Lord," he said, "the Jews are refusing to obey your laws!"

The king trusted Haman. He was shocked by these words. "Kill them all!" he commanded. So, orders were sent out that on a certain day every Jew was to be

Story

killed and no one must defend them. Haman made his magicians choose the best day for this dreadful event. So they cast lots, called 'purim'.

Mordecai told Esther about the king's terrible order and Haman's plan to attack all the Jews. He told her about the day chosen for the killing. He begged her to plead with the king to stop the attack.

"Only you can save us now," he said.

But how could she tell the king unless he asked her to speak? She would be sent away just like Vashti. Esther was afraid but she was also very brave. She fasted for three days to ask help from God. She begged Mordecai to ask all the Jewish people not to eat, also. Then she dressed in her finest clothes and went to see the king.

Esther's knees shook and her voice trembled with fear as she pushed through the crowd and stood before the throne. There was a terrible hush.

"I have come to ask a favour of you, my king," she said.

"How dare you!" screamed Haman. "Seize her!"

"Stop!" commanded Ahasuerus. He looked down at Esther from his golden throne. His new queen was defying him just like the last one! How could she do this, in front of all his subjects? The golden sceptre trembled in his hand.

And yet ... Ahasuerus looked deep into Esther's eyes. What troubled her so much that she should risk her life like this? His love melted the pride in his heart.

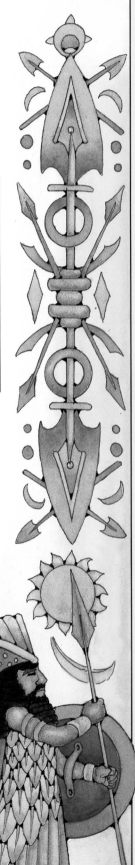

He pointed his sceptre at her.

"My Queen," he said, "your wish is my command."

"All I ask," spoke Esther softly, "is that you share a meal when I break my fast. I would like Haman to attend."

"Why hou have fasted, Esther?" asked Ahasuerus as they sat that evening, surrounded by courtiers, nibbling at the feast. The table groaned with exotic foods from all over Persia.

"There is evil amongst us, Sire," said Esther as she fed him succulent grapes.

"Someone here is plotting to murder all my people and I have fasted out of love for them."

"Who would do such a thing?" demanded the king. His eyes narrowed as he looked about the court.

"Haman," replied Esther. "He is doing this because he hates Jews."

"But, Haman has told me that Jews refuse to obey my laws! This cannot be allowed! They must die!"

Esther bowed her head and spoke softly. "Give me my life and the lives of my people. That is all I ask of you, O king!"

It was then that the king learned how Haman had lied about the Jews. He ordered Haman to be hanged. It was too late to stop the attacks on the Jews but the king sent messengers to warn them to fight back. So it was that on the 13th and 14th days of the month of Adar, the Jewish people won great victories.

In this way, because of the bravery of Esther, her people were saved and they rejoiced.

When Jesus was crucified

Jesus sat down for supper with his apostles, in a room in Jerusalem. He mixed wine with water in a cup. Then he said, "I want to celebrate this Passover meal with you before I suffer." He blessed the cup and passed it around. Suddenly he rose and began to wash the feet of his disciples.

They were shocked! Feet always became so dirty in the hot, dusty streets. But only slaves washed the feet of others. What could this mean? "You cannot do this!" they cried.

"If I cannot do this for you," said Jesus, "then you cannot be my people."

Jesus took some of the flat bread and gave a piece to each of his followers. He asked them to eat it. "This is my body," he said. Then he took a cup of wine and passed it around. "This is my blood," he said. "It will be poured out many times for the forgiveness of sins. Now, I shall eat and drink no more until the Kingdom of God has come."

Jesus knew this supper would be his last. He knew also that one of his followers was going to betray him. Jesus would be arrested.

And so it was. As they ate and talked and sang into the night, Judas Iscariot left the feast. Midnight came and Jesus knew there was no time left. He led his apostles out into the moonlight. They walked up to the Mount of Olives. Jerusalem lay like a city of dreams below them.

Not long afterwards soldiers burst into the supper room, searching for Jesus. He was not there. Up on the mountainside, in the Garden of Gethsemane, the apostles were afraid. Something was going to happen but they did not understand what it was.

"You will all leave me," said Jesus.

"Never!" they cried. But they fell asleep and Jesus was left alone to pray.

Suddenly, there was the sound of many footsteps. Judas led the soldiers into the garden. He went straight up to Jesus and embraced him.

"Greetings, Master," he said.

Jesus looked into his eyes. He knew this was a signal. "Do you betray the son of God with a kiss, my friend?" he asked. The apostles leapt forward to protect Jesus with their swords but he stopped them, saying, "People who live by the sword shall die by the sword."

Then the soldiers seized Jesus and the apostles ran away. He had told them they would desert him when he needed them.

So Jesus was led roughly away. Everyone knew that he was innocent. He had committed no crime but he was treated like a dangerous criminal. He was brought to see the high priests. It was against the law to pretend to be the King of the Jews.

One priest asked him, "Are you the Son of God?"

"Yes," said Jesus simply.

"Let the Romans send this man to his death," cried the priests. "Then no one in this country will believe he is the the Son of God!" So, Jesus was condemned to die. He was beaten by the soldiers. They made a crown from some thorny twigs and jammed this painfully onto his bleeding head. They put a red robe on him and placed a reed in his right hand as a sceptre and laughed at him, "Hail, King of the Jews."

Jesus was taken out of the city. Every condemned criminal had to be shamed in front of the people. Jesus had to carry the beam of the cross on his own back. He had become so weak from his beatings that the cross was too heavy for him. It was a painful journey to his death but Jesus refused any help. He was nailed to his cross. As the cross was pulled upright he suffered terrible pain. He hung between two common criminals. This moment is at the centre of what Christians believe. By dying like a criminal, Jesus paid the penalty for the wrong-doings of all of the human race.

"If he is the Son of God," said the priests as they watched him suffer, "then let him save himself."

Just then a terrible storm blew up and clouds blotted out the distant city. Jesus was taken down from the cross when it was certain he was dead. He was wrapped in linen cloths and placed in a simple tomb cut out of rock.

A great stone was rolled over the opening. It was all done in a great hurry, it was the Sabbath, a time when Jews were not allowed to work.

After sunset on the Sabbath, Mary Magdalene led some women to the tomb to prepare Jesus' body for a proper burial. They arrived at the tomb and found it open. The heavy stone at its entrance had been rolled away. The cave was empty. Had the body been stolen? Who would do such a cruel thing? They were filled with terror.

Just then a young man appeared before them. He was dressed in a white robe. He spoke to them. "Do not be afraid. Are you looking for Jesus? He isn't here. Why do you search for the living among the dead?"

Mary and her friends were afraid and ran away. They told the apostles what had happened but no one believed them. But they went back together to show them the tomb. Sure enough, the white linen cloths that had been wrapped around Jesus were there, but there was no body.

Mary Magdalene alone stayed near the tomb, sobbing, heartbroken. Then a figure appeared. It must be the gardener who was supposed to look after the tomb.

"Why are you weeping?" he said.

"Sir," begged Mary, "if you have removed the body, tell me where you have laid him and I will take him away."

"Mary," he said. At that moment she recognised his voice. It was the voice of Jesus. "Don't hold me back," he said. "I am going to my Father and your Father, to my God and your God. Tell that to the others."

Mary was overjoyed. She went back to the followers and told them that she had seen the Lord.

Think about these questions, and write just one sentence to answer each. Do not try to answer them all at once.

What is the most important thing you have learned about:

- prayers?

- what makes places special?

- holy places?

- celebrating Purim?

- celebrating Lent?

- rules that guide the lives of Christians?

- rules that guide the lives of Jews?

- Jesus?

- Israel?

- belonging to groups or communities?

- God?

- how people show that they believe in God?

- what it means to be a Christian?

- what it means to be a Jew?